TABLE OF CONTENTS

CHAPTER ONE

THE GOLFER IN MOTION

Golf is a unique athletic endeavor because players of all skill levels can compete against each other by using a handicap. Players also compete against themselves as they develop an improved handicap. For all players, regardless of actual golf ability, being able to compete in a meaningful match is a fantastic opportunity that does not present itself in any other sport.

However, we would all rather be the player with the lower handicap-prefer- ably with a constantly decreasing one at that! There are many ways to get better at the game of golf. We can improve the stroke with a putter or our ability to read putts correctly. We can improve our short game and iron play, and we can improve our game off the tee. The problem with these options is we need to be on a golf course to practice and improve. For most, it is difficult to find time to get on the course regularly enough to make substantial improvements in any of these areas, never mind all of them.

There is another option to improve your golf game. The world's best players have known for quite a while that the most effective way to improve a golf game is to improve the quality of the body playing the sport. As players earn better control of their bodies, it becomes easier to improve the technical part of their game because they now have more movement options available. Most players, whether they are high-handicap amateurs or those trying to keep their cards each year on the PGA Tour or

European Tour, struggle with one common issue: They are wasting precious time, energy, and confidence making technique changes when their bodies simply can't perform the desired movement. They are attempting to move the way their golf instructors believe would be benefi- cial, but the player may not have the physical skill set to do it. They may lack the mobility, strength, or body awareness to move in the direction, range, or sequence desired. The player may be suffering from an injury that prevents the desired position or perhaps has even become injured trying to force the body into a position it simply can't make, a common situation.

Sometimes a player will think he or she can move the required way, so he or she will spend time on the range, using significant energy, focus, and repetition to perform the desired movement without much attention to other variables (wind, water, etc.). Then the swing the player has practiced doesn't work on the course. In our experience, a player struggles to transfer a range swing onto the course because the player is attempting to use an unnatural or extremely difficult technique relative to the player's current physical skill set. When the physical skill sets improve, the technique becomes easier to pe rform, and the golfer is now able to take the range swing onto the course. If you have been practicing your swing technique but continue to struggle to find it on the course, you are most likely working on a movement innapprop riate for your current physical state. The most efficient way to improve technique and scoring will not be to continue beating balls on the range but instead to improve the body.

At profess ional golf tournaments, players often make the game seem simple, and their swings look effortless. The reality is that the game is far from easy, and their swings are anything but effortless. Great ball strikers such as Justin Rose, Graham DeLae t, Henrik Stenson, Kevin Chappell, Rory Mcilroy, and Lexi Thompson look like they are able to create tremendous dub-head speeds and still finish their golf swing with impeccable balance because they have put many hours of work into the technical aspects of the golf swing and the movement capacity of their bodies. The average golf fan is not able to appreciate just how much time these top players spend making sure their bodies are moving and functioning at the high levels necessary to consistently turn in a world-class performance.

It is no different from an F1 , NASCAR, or Indy Car being tuned up and modi- fied to meet the demands that each track will place on it. The world's fastest car with the world's best driver won't be able to compete at a championship level if the car doesn't have the proper tires for the track conditions that day.Each week on the PGA Tour, the manual and physical therapy section resem- blesa MASH unit, with many treatment tables set up and being used to fine-tune and patch the world's premier players. The fitness trailer doors are like turnstiles, given how many players pass through them as they strive to increase their on-course performances. Swing coaches meet with fitness trainers and manual therapists consistently to ensure they are teaching the most appropriate swing for their players based on each player's current physical state.

To teach or perform a golf swing, we are looking at improving the ability to perform movement. The golf swing requires more than 300 joints in the body to move through significant portions of their available motion and each one of the body's more than 640 muscles to perform at a h igh level to allow effective, repeated power and precision. The complexity of the golf swing is on par with that of some of the most difficult movements in sports, including Olympic liftsand gymnastics skills. The best movement coaches in the world must study diverse sciences, such as embryology, anatomy, cell biology, neurology, psychology, physiology, biomechanics, and nutrition, to help their players appropriately. This level of understanding takes years to accumulate, but our goal is to summarize these sciences in this second edition of Golf an atomy to help you streamline your journey, understand your body, and appreciate how to maximize your body's potential to move.

Success in sports often comes down to the athlete who can move more effectively than hisor her competitors. At its most fundamental level, prodigious movement requires an athlete to have both the ability to move and control movement at each joint through the required action. Many athletes, trainers, and coaches try to create effective movement without first gaining capacity in individual joints. This is analogous to attempting university-level calculus before learning how to count. You will probably get a few questions right on a multiple-choice exam, but you aren't going to see consistent results, and you're surely not going to see success over the long haul!

Once we have optimized the movement of our individual joints, we can develop a level of neurological contro l that allows the player to move into the positions they desire in the swing. Only then can we focus on gaining the strength and speed required for this sport. In the golf swing, this can be a lot of speed! After the 2017 Open Championship, Kevin Chappell improved his d river's club head speed from 119 to 121 up to 127 to 129 by the time he arrived at the World Golf Championship event a couple weeks later. He achieved this improvement by focusing on better body control and by making small changes to his technique to expose the new physical skill.

One of the biggest mistakes many golfers-and athletes in general-make when attempting to increase speed is failing to learn how to dissipate it. Decel- eration is more often the limiting factor in a golfer's quest for greater club-head speed than an actual lack of ability to accelerate or create speed. One of the nonnegotiable elements of any golf swing is that it must eventually end.

Many golf coaches working with young players now consider it paramount to teach their athletes to swing fast when they are young and then focus on technique later, once the potential to create speed has been developed. The reasoning is that technique can be taught anytime, but stimulating the nervous system to increase speed must be done during specific windows in an athlete's development. Although there is considerable evidence in the literature to back up this concept, this focus can be devastating to the long-term health of athletes if they do not take the steps necessary to ingrain adequate deceleration skills. Injury development will be more of a certainty than a possibility.

Our bodies are inherently intelligent and will attempt to minimize the likeli- hood of injury whenever possible. To appreciate what this means, let's consider our natural instincts if we were driving a high-end car and have 100 feet to stop before a hairpin-turn near the edge of a cliff. If we were driving with no brakes and really old, slick tires, we would absolutely approach that 100-foot mark with minimal speed. If we had brand-new brakes, new wheels, and an extra 50 feet of room to slow down, we would be much more likely to drive with considerably more speed because we would trust that the car and extra space would be sufficient to stop in time.

The new brakes and wheels are comparable to an optimized nervous system and healthy joints; the increased room to stop the car is equivalent to a body having an increased competence to move through greater motion with superior control. When we approach the end range of a joint's capacity, the soft tissues that support that joint must work at a much higher percentage of their maximum capacity to slow down the body segments. It is very easy to injure the joint and associated soft tissues (muscles, tendons, ligaments, joint capsu les) at the outer limits of a joint's motion. If we are able to earn even 10 percent greater mobility throughout our body's numerous joints, we would end up with a very large accumulated movement potential. More controllable movement equals greater space to slow down!

If you have more space to slow down and a greater ability to decelerate as a result of your training, you will, without question, have a much greater likelihood of increasing your club-head speed because your body will be more confident that it possesses the ability to stop the movement safely. Increased club-head speed equals greater distance, and greater distance with acceptable accuracy never hurts. Just ask DustinJoh nson, Rory Mcilroy, Jason Day, Adam Scott,Justin Thomas, Rickie Fow le r, and Jon Rah m. Oh yeah, they all happen to be among the top-ranked players in the world!

If you look at the top seven players from the PGA To ur's 2017 money list and compare their driving distance and their ranking for strokes gained on approach to the green and strokes gained putting (see table 1.1) when entering the Tour Championship, you can see how important it is to manage club-head speed and accuracy, both off the tee and when approaching the green.

CHAPTER TWO

TECHNIQUE

The golf teaching industry is a multibillion-dollar industry. Unfortunately, even this enormous monetary investment has done almost nothing to change the average North American handicap in the past 30 years. Most teaching for the golf swing has focused on attempting to change the motion of the golfer without improving the golfer's capacity to move. In addition, most golf teachers have very little, if any, understanding of anatomy, kinematics, joint capacity, or the common limitations that athletes of all skill sets experience. Without this under- standing, one can only guess at the technique a golfer can attain. However, as our good friends and successful PGA To ur coaches Sean Foley,

Drew Steckel, George Gankas, Scott Hamilton, and Mark Blackburn can attest, understanding the body and how it moves can help golfers make enormous improvements to their swing techniques quickly and safely. The guessing is significantly reduced when you know what an athlete is actually physically capable of achieving. If you know the golfer's feet, ankles, hips, spine, shoulders, and neck possess adequate mobility and the ability to move in association with each other in a way that fits a movement you would like them to do during the golf swing, you can be much more confident that you are not wasting their time or increasing the likelihood of injury.

Our goal for this second version of Golf Anatomy is to help change the way golf is taught at both amateur and professional levels. We want golfers reading this book to improve their bodies and increase their success in the short term and, just as important, increase the number of years they can play this great game at the highest levels of their ability, healthy and pain free. We want to stop the insanity so rampant in this sport of attempting to change the aesthetic product (the movement) without developing the quality of the underlying instrument (the body). The quality of your body will either enhance or inhibit your ability to create and replicate movement. Respect the complex motion of the golf swing. When it is performed freely and without hesitation or compromise, it is one of the most graceful yet powerful movements in sports. Some individuals will have more range of motion, and others will have rel- atively less. Kevin Chappell and Si Woo Kim are both world-class ball strikers. However, their swings look completely different because the potential for move- ment is different betwee n these two great players. If Kevin Chappell tried to swing like Si Woo, he would have no success. Si Woo's and Kevin's golf coaches both understand the golfer's body and its potential to move. This knowledge allowed them to streamline the technique they employed to best match the player's body. Fitting the technique to the body makes sense intuitively, yet most of us do not possess the knowledge to make this possible.

On the PGA Tour, coaches with players having a difficult time learning new techniques are one of our main referral sources. These coaches send us athletes because of our unparalleled track record for helping golfers progress their technique, which is secondary to cultivating the athlete's individua l movement potential.

How does improved body control lead to greater technique in less time and with less likelihood of injury? When it comes to identifying the perfect way to swing a golf club, the rapid advancement in technologies such as 3D video anal- ysis, radar, high-definition slow-motion cameras, and force plates revealed that there wasn't a specific, perfect way to swing a club. This applies to everyone. You ca n swing a club an infinite number of ways. Many end with the same result: The club face hits the ball squarely at impact.

The difference is the efficiency of the swing. If you

put Tiger Woods' swing in his prime against Graham Del aet or Henrik Stenson, or if you stack Hunter Mahan's swing on top of Jim Furyk's (he of the magical round of 58) swing, you would notice an incredible difference for much of the swing, but at impact, many of those differences would become less apparent. Obviously, all these players are phenomenal strikers of the ball, although their swing styles look completely different. They all have an efficient downswing that transfers a very high percentage of the energy produced during the downswing into the golf ball at impact. Their swings look different because the potential for movement within their bodies is different.

If you walk down a range at any PGA Tour golf tournament, you will notice that each player has a swing so unique that it's like a fingerprint. Yet when amateurs, and even many professionals, visit their local coaches, they are placed into a one-size-fits-all swing model that often does not work for the golfer who is trying to improve.

Comparing your swing with your favorite player's and attempting to mimic his movement is not a sensible way to improve the technical side of your full swing. The key is to make your body capable of producing the most efficient swing that you can produce. The future of golf no longe r relies solely on copying a standard swing. It is rather a meshing of proper mechanical technique and movement efficiency. Every player has a unique range of available motion in the joints, a unique level of strength, and inconsistencies with body awareness.

Only by maximizing his or her own physical profile can a player truly achieve optimal competence.

Each sport has its own specific demands, and golf is no exception. The fitness industry has finally moved past the archaic views of "exercise by body part" that anchored it down for the early days of professional training. Understanding body development during embryology and the concept of tissue continuity has finally allowed us to move past the prescription-by-body-part exercises and toward the prescription of movement and joint hea lth.

Golf Ana tomy provides the framework necessary to enable you to understand how joint mobility and health, body awareness, and balance are all prerequisites to greater full- body movements, the development of power, and a resilient body that resists injury.

We focus on some of the major pieces of golf fitness, including mobil- ity, balance and body awareness (proprioception), strength, and power. The order in which these specific components are trained is just as impor tant as the components themselves. The correct progression of exercises provides the most efficient training and diminishes the risk of injury. Training for power before you have obtained an adequate amount of mobility increases the risk of injury and results in minimal golf-specific performance expan- sion. This book will provide the essential skill sets to build a bulletproof golf body.

GENERATING POWER AND SPEED

At the sport's highest levels, it is increasingly common for players to ada pt their swings for improved efficiency in power generation. Our goals in Golf Anatomy are to introd uce exercises that will help you achieve greater golf fitness and to introduce some of the important principles used by today's top teachers and players when developing a technically efficient golf swing. Th ree of these principles are ground reaction force, the kinetic chain or web, and potential energy.

Ground Reaction Force

Generating speed using the arms creates many of the swing faults found on driving ranges. For maximal power creation with minimal negative stress on the body, the ground must be the first link in the chain of energy transfer. Newton's third law of motion states that for every force applied by one object onto a second, an equal and opposite force is applied from the second object back onto the first. For example , using the legs to drive forcefully into the ground results in the ground pushing back up with an equal force. The force the ground transmits into the golfer is known as the ground reaction force (GRF). GRF is then transferred up through the legs and into the pelvis. From the pelvis, the force is transferred into the golfer's core, shoulder complex, arms, and, finally, the golf club and ball. Transmitting this energy from the ground to the ball with the most efficiency creates the most power your body will allow.

Kinetic Chain or Web

The energy that stems from the GRF moves through the body in what is known as the kinetic chain or web. The different parts of the body act as a system of chain links, whereby the energy or force generated by one part of the body (or link) can be transferred to the next link. The optimal coordination (timing) of these body segments and their movements makes this transfer of energy and power up through the body efficient. Each movement in the sequence builds on the previous segme nt's motion and energy. The result of this transfer and summation determines dub-head speed. This kinetic chain connects adjacent join ts and muscles throughout the entire body via connective tissue. A weakness or injury in one area of the body impedes the transfer of energy. Weakness in this context can mean a deficiency in strength, range of motion, or body awareness. The body then compensates for this deficiency by overusing, or misusing, other body parts to try to make up for this lost energy. For an efficient golf swing in which the legs generate most of the power, large muscles contribute to force generation. When a weakness is present along the body's kinetic chain, the energy the legs produce cannot transfer effectively into the core and arms. As a result, the smaller muscles surrounding the area of weakness are placed under great stress. In time, this will lead to overuse injuries within the joints and soft tissues (the muscles, tendons, and ligaments) and make an efficient swing impossible.

Potential Energy

As with any sport, power can be improved by increasing the amount of poten- tial energy available. In the golf swing, potential energy is the energy stored within the body that can be used to create force. This is a very important con- cept because it highlights that improving movement ability directly correlates to power. Previously in this chapter, we discussed the importance of obtaining optimal joint motion at every level. We also mentioned how increasing each joint's movement just 10 percent would result in a large accumulation of move- ment potential throughout the swing. This is because increased mobility equals increased potential energy. As the golfer moves to the top of the backswing, he or she is creating potential energy within the body that can eventually be directed into the club head as the downswing leads to impact. Therefore, if a golfer is unable to move with a full range of motion, he or she is unable to capture maximal potential energy.

Potential energy is a perfect term because this storage of energy in the swing is only potentially transferred to the club head. In order to maximize the use of the potential energy stored in the back swing, the golfer must then be able to efficiently transfer the energy through the kinetic chain. This is why increasing mobility is useless, and sometimes harmful, unless it can be controlled prop- erly. A competent training program for golf must include both a way to increase mobility or potential energy and a way to contro l or direct it.

CHAPTER THREE

MAJOR MUSCLES AND JOINTS USED DURING THE GOLF SWING

The golf swing involves nearly every muscle and joint in the body, so it is very difficult to pick just a few to highlight as the most important. For simplicity, we have attempted to highlight a variety of the major muscles and joints utilized during the various subsections of the full golf swing. This list is not all-encom- passing but does provide a solid basis.

Upswing or Backswing

The upswing phase (figure 1.1), also known as the backswing, is performed with much less tension and physical stress throughout the body than the remainder of the golf swing. In this phase, balance, proprioception, and joint and muscle mobility are often more important than actual muscle strength. Having sufficient external rotation and retraction of the trail-side shoulder com- plex (the right shoulder in a right-handed golfer) and abduction, internal rotation, and protraction on the target side (the left shoulder in a right-handed golfer) while possessing sufficient internal rotation of the trail hip, exter- nal rotation of the target hip, and spinal rotation is more important than how strong the big muscle groups are. The problem with many golf fitness programs is the lack of time spent on increasing mobility or flexibility. If a golfer can't move into a desirable position while remaining in balance during the upswing, the remainder of the golf swing is negatively affected, regardless of the muscle strength or explosiveness of that athlete.

Although this phase of the swing uses mostly a golfer's mobility, some mus- cles provide a stable base so others can maximize their movements. During the upswing, the golfer must load the quadriceps, gluteus medius, and gluteus maximus in the trail leg and the obliques as the golfer coils toward the top of this phase of the golf swing. When these muscles work efficiently, the latissim us dorsi, infraspinatus, rhomboids, obliques, and multifidi can elongate properly to achieve the correct, full position of the upswing.

A great deal of time during golf lessons is spent on positions in the backswing. Average and even high-levelgolfers spend very little time on the downswing or follow-through. During fitness training, most golfers do not work on developing adequate motion throughout their bodies. However, many golfers may be unable to properly achieve the positions the golf teacher wants. When positive changes are not seen, the result is frustration for both players and teachers and may lead to injury and poor performance. When golfers increase their mobility to match the motion the instructor is trying to get them to create during the upswing, more time can be spent learning the downswing, impact, and follow-through phases of the swing.

Downswing

The transition from the upswing to the downswing requires great coordination and an ability to separate the lower body and pelvis from the upper body. The golfer initiates the transition between these two phases of the swing by moving the lower body into position to allow for the greatest muscle efficiency. One of the primary objectives is to position the tar- get-side knee over the outside aspect of the target foot. This puts the golfer in the proper alignment for the quadriceps and hamstrings to contract and straighten the knee, the gluteus maximus and hamstrings to contract and create hip exten- sion, and the muscles of the hip rotator cuff (piriformis, gluteus medius and minimus, and obtu- rators) to contract to create the initial external rotation of the

hip required to position the knee appropriately, provide lateral hip stability, and allow relative internal rotation of the hip joint, all on the targetside leg.

The trail-side leg uses the quadriceps, adductor magnus, hamstrings, gluteus maximus, and gastrocnemius muscles to create knee extension, hip extension, and ankle plantar flexion to help drive the golfer's weight onto the left side. The activation of the leg muscles helps drive the golfer into the ground and position the player so that the arms are able to move into position and create the desired angles of attack.

In the core, the obliques and psoas major are highly activated, creating a crunchlike position as the golfer's hips move through extension and the pelvis tilts in a relatively posterior fashion (the belt buckle starts to point up) while the chest remains over the ball. The target-side latissimus dorsi helps pull the golfer onto the target side while countering the force generated by the pectoralis muscles on both sides of the golfer's body.

Follow-Through

The follow-th rough move- ment in the golf swing (figure 1.3) allows the body- specif- ically the arms- to deceler- ate postimpact. This phase of the golf swing is very taxing because the muscles must work predominantly through eccentric contractions to slow down the body. The golfer's entire core- glutes, obliques, quadratus lumborum, psoas major, and transversus and rectus abdominis- works at maximum power to produce force and decelerate the body. The latissimus dorsi and the muscles that stabilize the shoulder blade to the spine and rib cage (serratus ante rior, rho mbo ids, leva- tor scapulae) as well as the muscles of the rotator cuff (sup raspinatus, infraspinatus, teres minor, subscapularis) help protect the shoulder join t from approaching its end range of motion under

High velocity.

UNDERSTANDING BODY AWARENESS

Often, body awareness, or proprioception, is the most overlooked sense. It is as important as the other senses for optimal athletic functioning, if not more important. The body uses proprioception to react with an immediate response to its surroundings. Your body must be able to respond rapidly to changing positions and different forces throughout the swing. Imagine how many body parts are moving in different directions during the golf swing, all in less than two seconds from the initiation of the upswing to the end of the follow-through. How can your body keep up with all that information? The body is able to do this through tiny sensory receptors in the muscles and joints that keep track of every joint position and stress throughout the body. The better these receptors work with their respective muscles, the more body awareness you will have throughout the entire golf swing. This will help you more frequently produce the correct movements and angles necessary for a good swing.

Kinesthesia is the ability to sense joint motion and acceleration. Proprioception and kinesthesia are the sensory feedback mechanisms for motor control and posture. The brain uses these feedback mechanisms to help orient the body and maintain balance as it evaluates a constant influx of sensory informa tion, sending immediate adjustments to the muscles and joints to achieve specific movement and balance.

Your ability to maintain balance under different circumstances depends on how well your body senses changes to body position and the forces applied against and within it. Walking, riding an escalator, and treading on uneven ground are some examples in which the body requires proprioceptive input to maintain balance during motion.

Training can lead to increases in muscular strength and increase the accuracy and speed with which the body is able to perceive and respond to various posi-tions and forces. Because improvements in balance and proprioception come through neural adaptation and often do not require an actual increase in muscle mass, these are often the first skill sets to improve once they are incorporated into a fitness program.

TRANSFERRING POWER

When a right-handed golfer initiates the downswing, the body weight often shifts to the target side (left side) when the golfer positions the left knee over the left foot. This places the golfer's lower body into an ideal force-generating position. With the knee over the foot, the quadriceps can straighten the knee, and the gluteus maximus and hamstring muscles can contract to create extension of the hip and pelvis. This combined extension movement drives the target foot into the ground.

The ground sends a resultant force back into the golfer that can be passed effortlessly through the legs and into the golfer's pelvis and core. If the pelvis and core are funct ionally strong and are able to move through the desired range of motion, the force will pass into the shoulder complex.

The shoulder complex consists of the muscles connecting the spine and ribs to the shoulder blade and the muscles connecting the shoulder blade to the arm. If the shoulder complex is functioni ng optimally, this force can be transferred into the arms and, finally,into compression of the golf ball. This comprehensive connection of joints and tissues highlights why fitness training for golf is so unique and cannot be done by isolating muscle groups.

In addition, using the legs to position the golfer and

create power helps minimize an over-the-top, slice-generating swing. We commonly see errors in understanding how the body moves toward the target in the downswing. For a right-handed golfer, it is common for coaches to refer to the pelvis moving left. For a player who has developed adequate physical skills, the focus should be on the left knee moving left so that it is positioned over the left foot. Then the athlete will automatically rotate the pelvis toward the target as the left knee and hip move into extension because the joints are aligned. When the player moves the pelvis to the left instead of the knee (often the left knee will be bent medially, or in a valgus position, compared to the pelvis and foot), the player will be pushed away from the target as the knee begins to straighten, and pelvis rotation will be restricted. The lateral shift of the lower body onto the targetside makes it much easier to bring the plane of the dow nsw ing forward toward the target. As such, the arc of the club will automatically have a more inside swing path.

When a golfer initiates the golf swing with her upper body, the angular momentum of the golf club forces the club head out away from the body on the downswing. Once initiated, this angular momentum provides resistance through inertia against the golfer's body, prevent ting the body from moving forward toward the target. Visually, you see a golfer who appears to have fast hips. The hips appear to rotate too quickly, which forces the club out and away from the body as the trail shoulder moves forward toward the ball, creating an over-the- top, slice-generating swing plane. Often a player like this is told to slow the hips down. Actually, the pro blem is not that the h ips are turning too fast but that the player is using the arms to generate the power and not using the legs to shift forward toward the target. When this player learns to use the legs to push into the ground, the apparently fast-rotating hips will appear to slow automatically, and the club head will begin to attack the ball from the inside more easily.

Players who appear to have fast hips and have trouble attacking the ball from the inside are rotating predominantly through the joints in the lower back with minimal rotation actually occurring at the hip joint. This lower-back-centered movement is especially stressful on the spine and supporting muscles. The wear and tear eventually

will lead to pain.

CHAPTER FOUR

TRAINING FOR SUCCESS

How can so many of today's top players, such as DustinJohnson, Justin Thomas, and Jordan Spieth, combine power and finesse in their golf swings? Part of the answer is obvious-their technique is world-class. The other part of the answer is not as obvious. They are able to move each part of their bodies through the required range of motion while maintaining kinetic balance, stability, and power. When one of these skill sets is limited, a golfer's efficiency in transferring energy is diminished, the golf swing suffers, and injuries occur. For this reason, each of these players puts a lot of time and effort into ensuring his body is in function- ally optimal form. This includes daily sessions in the

PGA fitness trailers during tournament weeks, regular treatment sessions for inju ry prevention and injury maintenance, and aggressive off-week fitness regimens.

Each week , these players include various forms of fitness in their routines: mobility exercises like those found in yoga, stability movements for the core and shoulder regions, balance and proprioception exercises, and strength and power movements. They use exercise equipment such as tubing and cables, medicine balls, stability balls, traditional weights, cardio equipment, and kettlebells. Many exercises require only body weight. It is important to use more than one type of training methodology in your golf fitness program to ensure a constant and progressive challenge to your body.

In many aspects of life, people tend to practice what they are good at and ignore what they find challenging or difficult. Decent ball strikers often spend most of their practice time beating balls on the range and almost completely ignore their short-game practice. The same occurs in the gym: People work on their strengths and ignore their weaknesses. For example, athletes who have poor flexibility often ignore or invest minimal time in a mobility program and spend most of their time executing traditional strength training exercises. The gains attained in the gym carry over only minimally onto the golf course. The result is frustration and a lot of wasted time.

Whether you are one of the golf wo rld's up-and-coming stars, an established veteran, or an amateur player looking to improve your game for future club rounds, using your time efficiently is impor tant. We all wish we had more time to do the things we love. Unfortunately, our time is limited, and we need to maximize the time we have. We chose the exercises in this book to maximize efficiency so that you quickly see results both on the course and in your daily life. Understand that fitness training for golf may be unlike any other training program that you have done. How much you sweat or how many calories you burn may not be the sole indicators of on-course improvement initially. The key concept is that you must improve your body for the demands of the golf swing, and that begins with proper mobility, balance, and proprioception. Be ready to train with a purpose, and eliminate any preconceived notions of what training should be. We developed Golf Anatomy to help you avoid the common pitfalls of fitness training.

Remember, different skills are involved in developing fitness. Often, athletes want to move directly from minimal or no specific fitness training to the most difficult or complicated movements, which leads to poor long-term performance gains and an increased likelihood of injury and mechanical restrictions. It is important to develop good balance, mobility, stability, and strength before attempting the power movements found in this book, in magazines, and on the Web. If you listen to your body and gradually progress through your exercise routine, you should see great improvements while staying safe and free of injury. In time, you will be able to expand your training routine and incor- porate the multijoint, complex movements found in the later sections of Golf An atomy.

Many of the legends of golf had problems with in jur ies toward the ends of their careers. Jack Nicklaus, Arnold Palmer, and Tom Watson all required hip reconstruction. Fred Couples and Tommy Armour III have had significant prob- lems with their backs. Tiger Woods has had significant injuries that challenge his ability to win not only a record number of majors but also potentially another tournament. Inju ries plague the golf world at a staggering level. It is common to see the members of a golf foursome, regardless of age or skill level, use a pain modulator, either before or after a round of golf. Many in juries th at require pain medication occurred off the course but limit the player's ability to play pain-free on the course.

Understand that injuries can also take place when you are involved in fitness training. Limiting the po tential for injury both on and off the course should always be a priority. The warm-up chapter has been included in this updated version so that you can improve your fitness level for golf without creating more opportunities for injury. It is always best to make sure your body is prepared for both workout and sport.

FITNESS PROGRAM DESIGN

The goal of Golf An atomy is to give you the basics for developing a golf fitness program specific to your needs. We decided not to include a detailed workout program in the first edition simply because each golfer's body is different. The exercises a golfer needs depend on what aspects of golf fitness need the most work.

Assuming a deficiency in all areas, it is best to focus workouts on mobility and proprioception, rather than on strength exercises. A standard workout template is not only impossible to create but also probably proves to be inefficient and detrimental for certain golfers. We encourage you to seek the help of a golf fit- ness professional in incorporating these movements into your current program. Having a proper comprehensive assessment from a golf fitness professional can help you understand how to efficiently create a program to maximize your gains. However, we understand that sometimes finding a qualified professional can be difficult. In chapter 8, we provide a few sample programs based on our work with professional golfers.

The exercises in Golf Anatom y appear in a specific order, one that provides the best opportunity to safely and efficiently build your body's movement potential. Many of the reader questions we received from the first edition of Golf Anatomy were about program design. How can Golf Anatom y be used to build an indi- vidual program? The reality is, we can't truthfully, or ethically, design a program or a style of program that would be adequate for all (or any) readers. When we design a program, it is typically centered around three premises:

1. Results of a comprehensive assessment

2. Specific training goals

3. Specific timing of the training program

When we create a program for a golfer, the first, and most important, step is always a comprehensive movement assessment. This allows us to understand how the player moves so that we can create a program specific to his or her strengths and weaknesses. This gives the player the most efficient workout pro- gram possible. It also prevents the athlete from training beyond his or her ability. Far too often , we see athletes who want to perform an intense workout but lack the skills required for basic movements. When strength is built on a poor foundation, it can only lead to poor swing habits, the inability to swing consistently, and eventually injury. Some athletes spend weeks focusing solely on mobility exe rcises, while others start their programming using more advanced exercises. Since we obviously do not have the luxury of a personal assessment within this book, we've written it in a specific order to provide some guidelines and make it a little easier for you to choose the exercises that are most appropriate for you. The second and third premises used in program design are a little easier to outline. Athletes often overlook or misunderstand the second premise, having a specific training goal. In this case, the training goal is to move efficiently and effectively throughout the entire golf swing. While it is more common to hear people say the goal is to hit the ball farther or more consistently, these are just side effects of creating a body that moves well in the golf swing. Although the goal of hitting the ball farther is a good one, it usually makes the athlete want to train with exercises geared solely around strength and power. Understand that hitting the golf ball well depends mostly on how well your body moves, not how strong you are. If you begin with getting your body to move efficiently and effectively throug hout the golf swing, you will be able to see why we wrote this book in this order and included these exercises. The third parameter in program design deals with the timing of specific work- outs. We will explain this later in the book, but it means that different fitness programs are appropriate depending on when they are used. Some programs are best for off-season training and others for competition weeks, preround, or a rehab, postinjury program. This becomes more important for the golfer who is competing professionally or consistently participating in tournaments. However, everyone should learn how to alter workouts from week-to-week if necessary. The workout you do the day before a big tournament is not the same workout you do a month away from competition.

Specific examples of programs are included later in this book. These pro- grams were used to help professional golfers who already possess an incredible amount of skill. Each program was designed differently because each player has a unique set of strengths and deficiencies in his or her movement, and the timing and goals of the fitness program had to be evaluated. You will notice that even top-levelgolfers so metimes, and oftentimes, need to focus mainly on skills involving mobility, balance, and proprioception to improve their golf game.

The first step in creating a fitness program is a proper warm-up. Chapter 2 pro- vides some relatively simple exercises to prepare your body safely and effectively for either a round of golf or the more intensive aspects of training. We recommend including a complete warm-up before any vigorous activity. The warm -up will incre ase your heart rate and respiration, which prepares your body to deliver oxygen and nutrients to the working tissues and eliminate cellula r waste. Your body temperature will increase slightly to encourage a more fluid environment within your connective tissue, in addition to many other physiological benefits. These physical improvements are important parts of a complete warm-up, but one of the most underappreciated aspects of a warm-up is the psychological benefit of preparing for the challenge ahead. Life is so busy these days. Most of us carry mental baggage to the gym and the golf course. We may have school, work, or family issues stealing our attention. The warm-up is a great opportun ity to gather your thoughts and focus on the upcoming task. When golfers come to the PGA Tour trailer for their preround warm-ups, it is common for them to talk about everything besides their training session or golf. By the time they finish their warm-up and leave the trailer, they have been able to decompress and gain the focus required to compete at the highest level. We often see amateur golfers skip their preround warm-ups and gym rats jump right to intensive training before they are physically and mentally prepa red. The first part of the round can be wasted as the golfer's body and mind adjust to meet the on-course demands,

And it increases the likelihood of injury both on the course and in the gym.

The next step is to figure out which exercises in this book you can initially include in your program. Trainers, therapists, and golfers often talk about athletes needing more stability or flexibility, but athletes generally need more mobility. Mo bility is the range of motion available that an athlete can control. In essence, mobility is the ability to stabilize your flexibility. Having the prerequisite mobility is fundamental to performing any exercise or sport technique effectively and efficiently. Devoting the most time to mobility (chapter 3), balance and propri- oception (chapter 4), and rotational resistance and deceleration (chapter 5) will lead to the greatest results in the long term for most athletes. Avoid the common error of rushing through the first chapters to get to the strength and power exercise chapters. While many people think these later chapters will yield the biggest rewards, the opposite often happens. Focus your initial time and effort on developing great body control, and you will find the remaining power and strength exercises will not only be much easier to perform but also much safer!

We suggest using the warm-up (chapter 2) and mobility (chapter 3) chapters as a mock assessment. If you have difficulty with many or most of these exercises, your initial program needs to focus entirely on these exercises. Alternately , if you are proficient with most of these exercises, you probably can incorporate more complex and difficult exercises from chapters 4 and 5 into your program. Typically, you will find that some movements are very difficult to perform while others are easier. Understand thatwhen you uncover weaknesses in your mobility and movement capabilities, these are precisely the things that you need to work on! Once you begin to gain proficiency with these exercises, you can progress to the later chapters of the book.

In addition to ordering the chapters in Golf Anatomy to create an athletic development program, we have placed the exercises in each chapter so that they build on the skill and experiences of the preceding exercises. This will help you create a program that fits your specific needs.

Golf is a wonderful activity that can contribute to a healthy lifestyle byencour- aging both increased physical activity and social interaction. We truly hope that Golf Anatomy will help increase your enjoyment on the course through improved functional capabilities and a decreased likelihood of on-course injury and dis- comfort. But more important, we hope that it leads to better scores on the course!

PREWORKOUT WARM-UP

Whether you are preparing for a round of golf, a pickup game of soccer, or a difficult training session in the gym, you need to include a proper warm-up. While a warm-up may vary depending on the activity, the goal is the same: to move all the necessary joints, asso ciated muscles, and con nective tissue through a full range of motion in multiple planes of movement. A proper warm-up primes the mechanoreceptors in the joints, muscles, and conn ective tissues throughou t the body. These mechanorece ptors provide the brain with information detail- ing the positions and forces the body is experiencing. The brain translates this information to make informed decisions about the speed, force, and direction of movement needed to best allow the intended action to occur. Cold tissue isn't as responsive as warm tissue due to the colloid quality of connective tissue. Therefore the warm-up is key to preparing the body for action, encouraging the mechanoreceptors to begin signaling the brain so the brain can create and respond to movement accurately and quickly. Moving the joints through a full range of motion and multiple planes of movement increases the number of receptors activated. The more active receptors, the more information the brain receives, lead ing to a greater likelihood of success and redu ced risk of injury. The athle te's ability to use this fu nctional range of motion effectively will be addressed in chapter 3, which is about mobility, but before then, the warm-up should prepare each joint complex for its full range of motion.

The true goal of any athlete should be to increase the range of motion of the joint complexes while maintaining complete control. While lack of mobility is a problem for any athlete, excessive uncontrolled mobility is equally detrimental. We often tell our athletes that our job is to help them increase range of motion, but once we do that, we must immediately follow with exercises and movement patterns that help control this newfound movement. Once you develop your body's awareness of these important joint comp lexes and act ivate the kinetic web by wor king the joint at both its shortened and lengthened positions, you can begin to incorporate each segment into multijoint and full-body movements that progressively increase the demands placed on your motor control.

WARM-UP PROGRESSION

The way we approach the warm-up is just as important as the order in which we train for golf. We will begin with the feet because this area must function well for us to have any chance of successfully perfo rmin g movements that involve our feet on the ground. Our feet anchor our bodies to the ground and provide feedback about the surface on which we move. The muscles and connective tissue (joint capsules, ligaments, tendons, and fascia) in the feet and ank les are loaded with mechanoreceptors. Mechanoreceptors are the sensory receptors that the body uses for balance and body awareness. The rest of the body's joints position themselves large ly as a resu lt of the information the mechanoreceptors of the feet and ankles obtain.

If you perform an exercise such as a squat but do not have the necessary mobility in your feet and ank les, you will require much greater movement from other joints , such as the hips and spine, to compensate for the deficiency in the feet and ankles. This greatly increases the opportunity for injury and the like- lihood that you will be unable to complete the movement. Ensuring that each joint complex is functioning at the greatest capacity before attempting more difficult and demanding tasks that require the integration of the body's kinetic web is important.

Once we have developed the muscles and joints in the feet and ankles, we will move up the kinetic chain and focus on increasing the range and control in the hips. Having an appropriate range of hip mobility can allow the lower back to perform the role it is best suited for. One of the most common reasons golfe rs deve lop lowe r back pain or injury is a loss of hip mobility, specifically internal rotation and adduction of the lead hip, external rotation and abduction of the trail-side hip, and extension of both hips.

When the hips are not able to move through the transverse plane into internal and external rotation appropriately, the lower back will be forced to pick up the slack and rotate. The facet joints of the lower back are anatomically positioned to encourage flexion (bending forward) and extension (bending back) and not rotation. When excessive rotation occurs, the greatly increased shear forces on the intervertebral discs lead to wear and tear of the annular fibers of the discs and joints. Lowe r back extension and rotation has been shown to increase the stress on the facet joints, specifically on the trail side, in golfers. Maintaining the correct le vel of mobility in the fee t, ank les, and hips keeps you less dependent on the back to produce rotation, and you will be able to repeat your golf swing more dependably and play for more year's injury free.

Many of us cannot properly segment the spine, which is the ability to move each of the spine's 24 presacral vertebrae (lumbar, thoracic, and cervical) through a full range, both in isolation and in conjunction with the other joints in the preworkout warm-up 21 Spine. When an athlete cannot purposefully move the individual segments in his or her spine, the player moves a block or group of segments together. A hinge involves excessive motion at one segment to compensate for the Lack of motion occurring at its neighboring segment. This results in increased strain and less efficient movement in that part of the spine.

Most common ly, we see the middle and upper thoracic spine and the lower lumbar spine not moving segmentally and instead moving as a block. In addition, the main contributors to degeneration or arthritic changes in the body are a lack of movement or excessive movement. When a joint does not move (an area of the spine unable to segment), we begin to see arthriticchanges develop because the body no longer deems these segments necessary for normal daily function. After working on the individual joint comple x's movement, you can begin to incorporate them into integrated movements with the confidence that your joints will perform to the greatest of their abilities. We initially begin this integration of joint complexes through controlled movements and then progress to more dynamic movements that involve moving through multiple planes, ranges, and speeds. Upon completion of this warm-up and joint health section, you will be

prepared to move into the more intensive mobility section in chapter 3.

ANKLE DORSIFLEXION USING

SUPERFLEX BANDS

Execution

Loop or tie one end of a band around an immovable object. Place the other end aro und your right foot at the lowest part at the front of your ankle. Turn your back to the object holding the band so the band is behind you. Assume a split sta nce, with your right foot slightly forward. Stand far enough away from the anchor point to allow medium to heavy pressure to build in the band. Push your right knee forward as far over your toes as you can without lifting your heel at 30 percent maximal force and hold for 60 seconds. Release the knee to return to the start position and then perform a second repetition. Repeat on the left side.

Muscles Involved

Primary: Gastrocnemius, soleus, Achilles tendon

Secondary: Flexor hallucis longus, flexor digitorum longus

HIP 90/90

Execution

Sit on the ground. Put your left thigh out in front of you with the knee bent 90 degrees and the outside of your left thigh and leg flat on the ground. Bend the right knee 90 degrees and point the right thigh and knee directly to your right. Place your left hand on the ground to your side for support and stability. Align your spine and torso with your pelvis. Position the spine upright so you feel tension in your right hip joint, but not your lower back. For most people, this means the spine will be somewhat tilted to the left. Squeeze your right glutes to push the right hip forward until you feel pressure in your right hip. Push your right knee, shin, and ankle (equally for all three) into the ground with 30 percent of your maximal effort. Hold this pressure for 60 to 90 seconds. With- out shifting your body, attempt to reduce the pressure under your right shin by pulling the leg away from the floor. Hold for 15 to 20 seconds. Switch legs and repeat on the other side.

Muscles Involved

Primary: Piriformis, gluteus medius, gluteus minimus, hip capsule ligaments

Secondary: Adductors (right side)

PIGEON POSE

Execution

Begin on all-fours. Slide your right knee forward so that your thigh and knee are directly in front of your hip socket and the outside of your right thigh is touching the ground. Place your right foot comfortably near your left thigh. Attempt to straighten your left leg. Keep your pelvis level and pointing directly forward. Place your hands on the ground and keep the torso long from your tailbone to the top of your head. Hinge at the hip until you feel a moderate stretch in the back of your right hip. Don't move your torso as you press your right thigh into the ground with 30 percent maximal pressure. Hold for 60 seconds. Do not move your torso as you try to pull your right shin off the ground. You won't be able to lift the shin, but try to feel the tension build between your abdominals and inner thigh. Hold this tension for 15 to 30 seconds. Repeat on the opposite side.

Muscles Involved

Primar y: Psoas major Oeft side), hip capsu le (right side), piriformis (right side), quadratus femoris

Se condary : Rectus femoris, rectus abdominis, gluteus maximus (right side), gluteus medius (right side)

TRIANGLE POSE

Execution

Stand in a staggered stance with your feet 3 to 4 feet apart, left foot in front and pointing forward. Lift your arms straight out to your sides so they are parallel to the ground. Push your left knee forward so that it is in line with your left foot. To rotate your torso, reach up with your right hand while reaching down with your left hand. Keep your right hand, right shoulde r, left shoulder, and left hand in line with each other at all times. Maintain your rotation as you slowly straighten your left knee. Straighten the knee only as far as you can maintain the torso rotation. Hold this position for up to 60 seconds while trying to main- tain pressure from the left foot into the ground and keeping your spine straight and long. Slowly return to the start position by reversing rotation. Repeat on the other side.

Muscles Involved

Primary: Adductor longus, gracilis, pectineus, latissimus dorsi, external oblique

Se cond ary: Gluteus medius, gluteus maximus, tensor fasciae latae

SEGMENTAL CAT CAMEL

Execution

Kneel with your hands and knees on the floor. Ro und your spine as much as possible, so your back forms a smooth curve and both your head and pelvis are tucked under into maximal spinal flexion. You should feel engagement throughout your core to keep your pelvis tucked under your body. Try to tilt just your pelvis as you keep the rest of your spine rounded. Slowly work your way up your spine, trying to move only one segment at a time into extension. Do this by pulling one vertebrae down toward the floor until it feels like it locks out and then move up to the next segment. Keep the remainder of your spine flexed as much as possible. Once you have reached the top of your back, lift the head while keeping your chin tucked. Untuck your chin and look up to the ceiling to move the very top segments of your spine. Slowly reverse the steps to return to the start position. Each pass up and down the spine should take 30 seconds per direction. Perform 3 repetitions.

Muscles Involved

Primary: Erector spinae (iliocostalis , longissimus , spinalis), interspinalis , spinal ligaments, rectus abdominis

Se cond ary: Rhomboids, pectoralis minor, longus colli, Iongus capitis

SCAPULAR CIRCLES

Execution

Stand with a small weight in your right hand. Try to crush the weight by squeezing your hand as hard as possible while building tension in your legs and core. Mainta in this tension throughout the exercise. The only part of your body allowed to move during this exercise is your left shoulder blade. Slowly pull your left shoulder blade down toward your butt as much as possible. Next, pull the left shoulder blade toward your spine and then keep the blade pulled as tight toward the spine as possible as you slide it up as high toward your ear as possible. Keep your left shoulder blade as high as possible while moving the blade out to your side, away from your spine. Once your shoulder blade moves away from the spine, lower it back down toward your butt. Each circle should take at least 20 seconds. Perform 5 repetitions and then switch sides.

Muscles Involved

Primary: Rho mboid major, rhombo id minor, serratus anterior, subscapularis, levator scapulae, latissimus dorsi, middle and lower trapezi us

PRONE SWIMMERS FOR SHOULDERS

Execution

Lie on your abdomen with both hands palms up and resting on your lower back. A pillow or pad under your chest may make it easier for you to keep your neck in line with the rest of your spine. Squeeze your shoulder blades together. Lift your elbows as high as possible. Lift your palms toward the ceiling and straighten your elbows. Keep your hands and elbows as high as possible throughout the exercise. Slowly begin to move your arms out to your sides. When you get to around shoulder level, pull your shoulder blades back and down toward your butt as you rotate your arms so that your knuckles are now facing up toward the ceiling. Hold this position for 10 seconds and then reverse the steps until you return to the start position. Repeat 2 more times.

Muscles Involved

Primary: Rhomboids, lower and middle trapezius, serratus anterior, latissi- mus dorsi

Se cond ary: Infraspinatus, posterior deltoid

ABDOMINAL PLANK

Execution

Lie face down with your arms bent close by your sides. Lift your body off the ground, using your forearms and toes to support yourself. Tighten your abdom i- nals and keep your spine straight without allowing your lower back to sag toward the ground. Your elbows should be under your shoulders and your palms flat on the ground. Continue looking down at the floor during the exercise so that your entire spine is straight. Don't forget to breathe while holding the position. Hold for 15 to 30 seconds. Repeat 2 or 3 times.

Muscles Involved

Primary: Transversus abdominis, rectus abdominis, internal oblique, external oblique

Secondary: Lower back extensors, serratus anterior, and psoas major

SINGLE-LEG STANCE HIP FLEXION AND KNEE EXTENSION

Execution

Stand on your right foot. Keep your right knee as straight as possible and your spine as tall as possible. This is good posture for this exercise. Place a small, light ball between the top of your left thigh and your lower left abdominals. Try to pop the ball as you pull your knee as close to your chest as possible while maintaining good posture. Maintain the compression on the ball as you slowly straighten your left knee. Straighten the knee only until you begin to lose the height of the knee or compression of the ball. You will not be able to straighten your knee all the way if you are pulling your knee up as high as possible. Per- form 10 to 15 slow knee extensions in good posture and then switch legs.

Muscles Involved

Primary: Hamstrings (semitendinosus, semime mbranosus , biceps femoris), psoas major, rectus fe moris, gluteus maximus

Secondary: Adductor magnus

30 degrees backward.

THREE-POSITION SIDE LUNGE

Execution

Stand on your left leg with your right foot just off the ground. Step directly to your right with your right foot approximately double shoulder-width. As your right foot hits the ground, push your right knee out to the side over your right foot (don't let the knee collapse in) and press your hips back and down. Your left knee should be straight. Push your right foot into the ground to drive your- self-up and return to the start position. Repeat, but this time step approximately 30 degrees forward with your right foot instead of directly to your side. Re peat again, but this time step approximately 30 degrees behind the original step. Repeat each of these positions 5 times and then switch sides.

Muscles Involved

Primary: Adductor longus, adductor magnus, gluteus maximus, quadriceps (rectus femoris, vastus lateralis, vastus medialis, vastus intermedius)

Secondary: Hamstrings (semitendinosus, sernimembranosus, biceps femoris)

STRENGTH FOR INCREASED DISTANCE

Determining the level of strength a player must have to play his best is difficult. Some of the longest hitters on the PGA Tour would not be considered overly impressive in the weight room, yet smaller players, such as Justin Thomas and Rickie Fowler, are still able to create incredible club speeds and move the ball long distances. What makes this possible? Other players, such as DustinJohnson and

Bubba Watson, are able to use their long limbs and levers to use physics and geometry to create high dub-head speeds. DJ looks at home in the gym while Bubba does not. By contrast, Rory Mcilroy, Jason Day, Jordan Spieth, and Kevin Chappell emphasize the gym in their training programs to help minimize the stress of the golf swing on their bodies and get a competitive edge with the ability to smash the ball out of the rough when required.

In over a decade working on the PGA Tour, we have seen the positive effects of strength training on player performance. However, some players focus heavily on a strength-based program and improve dramatically in their gym performance but see minimal improvement on the golf course. In some extreme cases, players lost distance and suffered more regular injuries after performing a strength-focused training program. Why do some players excel and other fail when it comes to using strength training to improve on-course capability and performance?

In most cases, the answer is surprisingly simple. Players who have seen incredible success after focusing on a strength-based training program had pre- viously, or simultaneous ly, deve loped the required mobility, body awareness, and neurological control necessary to perform strength-based exercises properly and allow movement through the preferred range of motion in the golf swing. The players without successful carryover of strength training did not. The category of forme r PGA Tour players is littered with golfers who tried to improve them- selves in the gym but did not appreciate the necessity of building a compe tent base of mobility and body control before focusing on strength enhancements. Many of these players developed injuries and regressed or merely maintained their levels of performance.

Golfers can be above average in strength in the gym while training with machines or free weights, but if they are not able to transfer that gym strength to the golf course, they are wasting a great deal of the time they spend on fitness. Traditional bodybuilding has little to no place in developing a strong body for golf. It is focused too much on individual muscles and not on movement.

The brain stores movements at a much greater capacity than it stores the understanding of individual muscles. When specific areas in the brain are acti- vated or signaled, a motor program (movement) occurs. Athletic movements and daily activities require multiple areas of the body to work simultaneously or in coordination, so traditional body-part focused training has little place in an athletic training program.

Additionally, most traditional strength and power training programs involve the arms and legs moving together in the same direction and with the same joint angles. Upper body examples include the bench press, pull-up, pull-dow n, triceps pull-down, and dip. Each exercise requires a stable or stiff thoracic spine to support the movement. The problem is very few athletic scenarios require a stiff thoracic spine with both limbs moving in the same way. Throwing a ball, taking a golf swing or a shot in hockey, swinging a bat, run ning, and throwing a punch all involve the athlete's thoracic spine moving (flexing, extending, rotating) to effectively position the extremities while one arm pulls and the other arm pushes. Traditional training exercises do not encourage this type of movement among the affiliated joint complexes. In fact, these exercises promote the opposite pattern, and the result can often be seen in the stiff gait exhibited by long-time gym rats who walk with almost no motion in the trunk and with an arm swing isolated to the glenohumeral joint (shoulder).

We are not saying that muscle strength does not matter, but if the individual muscles cannot communicate and work with each other, that strength will be useless in a golf swing. For this reason, it is crucial to formulate your fitness routine with exercises that not only improve individual muscle strength but also improve the way muscles work together. This is what we mean by creating functional strength and not just raw strength (figure 6.1).

With a progressively younger, more athletic, and better-trained athlete becoming the norm on the PGA Tour, a golfer's body has to move as well as possible to keep up. One of the main reasons 40-year-oldHe nrik Stemson was able to win a legendary duel with 46-year-old Phil Mickelson at the 145th Open Championship was because of the priority both players placed on their bodies for years before competing in that major championship.

These two athletes illustrate one of our observations over a decade of working on the PGA Tour: Proper mobility and body awareness are an important part of an athlete's training program.

To be truly strong in golf, you need strength through the entire range of motion involved during the golf swing. A weakness at any joint through any section of the motion will create a breakdown in the golf swing. Lifting weights in one plane using a bench or traditional machines greatly limits the functional strength you can develop and eliminates the need for your body to create and maintain stabilization through a full range of motion while performing an exercise. This ability to stabilize the body while in motion is needed in golf and therefore must be heavily incorporated into your exercise routine.

With this as part of your strength training focus, the strength you gain in your fitness training begins to have a much greater carryover to the golf course.

For this reason, we have formulated this chapter to include exercises that expand on movements and concepts described in the previous chapters and combine them into more functional movements. The exercises in this chapter should be performed only when the exercises in the mobility, balance and proprioception, and rotational resistance and deceleration chapters can be completed comfortably and with good form. If you have already developed the prerequisite level of body control and are able to perform the exercises in the strength and power chapters easily, you are sure to see incredible benefits after the movements in this chapter are incorporated into your training program.

Many people think that golfers do not need to be strong since they are not running, jumping, or knocking over other people. This attitude is probably because the word strength typically con jures up images of a guy with huge muscles benching 300 pounds (135 kg) in the gym. Although this is one form of strength, there are many othe rs. We have already explained that golfers require fun ctional strength to perform at the highest levels. There is also another key reason that strength is important: injury preve ntion.

The average person would never associate golf with injury. However, as all professional golfers and avid amateur players know, injuries are prevalent throughout the sport and in fact are almost inevitable. The statistics on in jur ies at the to uring level are staggering. About half of all touring professiona l golf- ers will have some injury each year that will cause them to miss many weeks of golf. Of those playing, up to 30 percent are actually playing injured. Those num bers are very high, and any injury in a given year can be the difference between keeping the tour card or not. For touring professionals, the tour card is their job ticket. Lose the card, lose the job. For nonpro fessional golfers, an injury may mean missing many months of golf or, even worse, deciding to quit golf altogether. For these reasons alone, you should increase your golf strength so you can prevent injuries as much as possible.

Two types of injuries occur in golf: connective

tissue and muscle injuries. Although there are no heavy loads to carry or move in golf (unless you are a caddy!), very high forces develop because of the speed of the swing. The mus- cles and joints not only help create these forces but also must be able to gen- erate opposing forces to slow down and ultimatelystop the swing. As muscle strength- both individual and functional- increases, so does your ability to withstand the forces in the golf swing. If you do not possess adequate strength and resiliency in the muscles and connective tissue to create and slow down these forces, then injury is sure to occur. By properly incorporating the exercises in this chapter into your exercise program, you will see rapid improvement in both your confidence and physical competence in your golf swing. As an added bonus, you avoid taking time off because of injuries, which would slow down the progression of your game. As your success with these exercises improves, so will the ease with which you are able to control your body on the course. Become fu nctionally strong and you will become golf strong!

Initially perform the following exercises with a load that allows 8 to 12 repeti- tions. For exercises that require resistance tubing, cable machines, or free weights, start with a low resistance that allows you to complete 3 sets of 12 repetitions per set. When you can complete 3 sets of 12 repetitions, increase the resistance or weight and complete a lower number of repetitions, but be sure you are able to maintain appropriate form throughout. For exercises that require only body weight, begin with

2 or 3 sets of 6 to 8 repetitions. Once you can easily complete 3 sets of 8 repetitions, increase to 10 repetitions. Some exercises may require other ranges of repetitions. In these cases, the number of repetitions is included with the exercise instruction.

CHAPTER FIVE

PROGRAM PLANNING

Since training programs need to be designed specifically for each golfer, based on his or her needs, desires, limitations, and gifts, we analyzed the fitness pro- grams of some of the world's best golfers to see how they use the exercises in Coif Anatomy during different phases of the season. The selection of exercises obviously changes based on the on- and off-course demands of the individual athlete and the accumulated stress that player has been exposed to. Additionally, the level of resistance, number of sets, rest periods, and other parameters these athletes use change day to day and week to week and depend on that athlete's biometrics, recovery, and so on.

Unfortunately, in most cases, an athlete begins working with us due to an injury or significantly limited body control. Consequently a program often begins with an emphasis on improving the quality of movement and control in indi- vidual joints. Healthy, functional joints are non-negotiable. It's unreasonable to expect a joint to magically attain the range of motion required to safely perform a complicated multijoint movement if it can't create or control an equal or greater range of motion when performing a simple single-joint movement. Yet many trainers, athletes, and coaches seem to have this expectation.

When the athlete has earned the prerequisite joint heal th and motor control, the focus of the program usually shifts to overall body awareness and movement efficiency. We emphasize improving the function and control of the feet, hips, spine, and shoulder complexes. We need our athletes to own the ability to move each of these areas segmentally, in isolation from neighboring joint complexes. Once they have this level of neurological control, we incorporate these joints into more complex movements that use multiple segments in a coordinated manner. Who would have an athlete do a power snatch without the necessary ankle dorsiflexion, hip hinge, or ability to perform a body weight squat? In Golf Anatomy, we suggest incorporating the movements described in the mobility and balance and proprioception chapters (chapters 3 and 4) to build a foundation that you can use as you progress to the strength and power chapters.

This chapter describes portions of programs used by Lydia Ko, Gary Woodland, Kevin Chappell, Graham Del aet, and Byeong-hun (Ben) An. Lydia's program focuses on the exercises she used to build a strong foundation from the feet up as she earned the control of each body segment. Ben's program is an example of what he did in the week before his playing season. He had already built his overall strength and power capacity during the offseason, so he tapered and focused on recovering for the heavy travel requirements that go with playing on both the European and PGA Tours. Graham Delaet used this portion of his program to maintain a healthy and functional body after back surgery and minimize the effects of the surgery. Kevin

Chappell's program is an example of a typical preround warm-up session. This program helps ensure his body is properly prepared, whether this is Kevin's first or fifth week in a row playing on the tour.

Lastly, Gary Woodland's program shows how he built his overall capacity in the middle of his off-season. Unlike many of the other programs in this chapter, Gary's program included more exercises from the strength and power chapters of this book. He already built his basic capacity and focused on building strength and transitioning to a power-focused block in his training. Most athletes playing on the world's top tours do not spend a significant amount of time in this section of their programming because there isn't enough of an off-season , and many athletes need to focus on recovery for a good chunk of their time off. When Gary performed a strength or power-focused block in his training, there was an equal emphasis on body recovery. This may include soft tissue treatment, cryotherapy, acupuncture or dry needling, hyperbaric therapy, or other treatments.If you are going to train hard and break the tissues down, you need to ensure the tissue has the environment necessary to allow appropriate recovery to occur.

Pain and inflammation are probably the greatest impedime nts to reaching an ultimate level of performance, whether in an elite athlete or a weekend warrior. Pain and inflammation patches may be the safest method to help provide relief for musculoskeletal conditions, from golfer's elbow to lowe r back pain, from shin splints and irritated meniscus to shoulder and neck pain.

FOCUS ON MOBILITY, BALANCE, AND PROPRIOCEPTION

If working on your fitness is a new experience for you or if you are coming back to fitness after a significant time away, we highly recommend spending time on the warm-up, mobility, and balance and proprioception chapters (chapters 2, 3, and 4). For most golfers, the exercises in these chapters provide the most value in terms of health and on-course performance. Each individual will have a different past when it comes to injuries, train ing experience, genetics, and health. If you require greater mobility or strength in the arms and shoulders, spend more time on these exercises. If you strugg le with foot or hip mobility, put more emphasis on these exercises in your programming.

Lydia Ko's program (table 8.1) is a great example for the golfer who is just beginning a training program and needs to improve mobility in the feet, hips, spine, and shoulders. In Lydia's program, the exercises focus on isolating individual joint segments to acquire the ability to move them against a neighboring segment with control. Most of us are not able to consciously move an individual joint segment in isolation. As a result, we are forced to use compensatory and inefficient coup led motion that places more stress on the muscles and connective tissues throughout the body. Once these key areas become more mobile and can be controlled with greater accuracy, you can begin to combine the body parts into more complex multijoint movements.

When Lydia first began working with Dr. Davies, many of the essential elements of the program were a challenge for her. In the past, she attempted more complex exercises before developing the prerequisite control of her body instead of building a foundation on more fundamental movements. This created poor movement patterns that were difficult to correct. You will notice that this program places significant e mphasis on cultivating balance and body aware- ness. Ultimate ly she quick ly mastered these exercises and advanced to more multifaceted movements.

I never appreciated how important it was to gain

control of each area of my body. When I focused on this in my training, it became pos- sible to maximize the efficiency and the precision of my movement during the golf swing. TI1e greatest piece of advice I can offer you is to master the basics because the basics are what all the other skills develop from.

Lydi a Ko

FOCUS ON STRENGTH AND MOBILITY THROUGH BODY-WEIGHT EXERCISES

Once you can move each joint through the necessary range of motion under the desired control, move to more complex exercises using your body weight. If you don't have significant internal and external rotation of the glenohumeral joints (shoulders), your shoulder blades can't protract and retract properly, or your thoracic spine can't extend, flex, and rotate sufficiently, do not perform crab to beast transitions. If you have developed the required motion in these joints, moving to a more demanding task is encouraged.

The program used by Byeong-hun (Ben) An (table 8.2) provides a great exam- ple for the type of exercises that could be selected once sufficient control has been obtained at each individual joint. Ben's body-weight-dominant program is quite challenging but can be made more or less difficult by increasing or decreasing the number of repetitions performed. Ben's well-balanced program will strengthen the legs, arms, and trunk through all planes of motion while also improving mobility througho ut the body.

When Ben began working with Dr. Davies at the 2016 Masters, he was not able to hit a single full shot in a practice round of that tournament because of a neck injury that he had been dealing with leading up to that week. Unfor tu- nately, the injury developed into a significant problem the week before Augusta and impeded his ability to swing a club. He was able to tee up on Thursday, and although it was a struggle, he was able to stay within reach of making the cut with a strong performance on Friday. He played beautifully on Friday but ended up missing the cut by one. He learned that the pain and dysfunction in his neck was due to a lack of control in the extension and rotation of his tho-racic spine and the movement of his shoulder blades. As a result, shoulder and arm movements were placing significantly more stress on the neck and upper back than should have been necessary. Now that he moves with greater profi- ciency and has developed the prerequ isites to more complex exercises, he can perform strength exercises with less negative stress to his body. This benefits his performance and reduces the opportunity for injury! In be n's program (table 8.2), you can see some of the exercises he was doing the week before starting the 2018 season. He had already put two months of work into developing his overall strength and power and was tapering his training and maintaining his movement potential while developing his energy reserves before starting a busy schedule playing on both the European Tour and PGA Tour.

I worked hard to improve the control of my body

and experienced a significant improvement in my club-head and ball velocity as a result. I never would have though t that learning how to move my body more efficiently would enable me to hit the ball so much further.

FOCUS ON POWER AND STRENGTH

When advanced body-weight exercises can be performed properly, it is appro- priate to add an external resistance (dumbbells, kettlebells, etc.). You can emphasize improvingstrength and then power. Gary Woodland's program (table 8.3) shows the type of programming he did in his off-season after he prepared his body appropriately using body-weight exercises to improve his mobility and body awareness. This program, which he performed after going through a full warm-up, emphasizes power exercises initially and then strength-based training (trap bar deadlift) so the nervous system isn't fatigued when there are high demands on deceleration and acceleration, as experienced in the power that stresses both power and strength.

The 2017 season was the first time that Gary Woodland played a complete season on the PGATour and remained injury-free. Much of this success was due to a new emphasis on maintaining his fitness training throughout the season when he would have historically fallen off a little as a result of the distractions that present themselves on tour. This new training regimen was helpful, and he integrated a regular treatment and recovery program. Since Gary was able to finish the 2017 season healthy, he was able to use the 2017-2018 off-season as an opportunity to focus on improving his strength and power capabilities. This program is an example of the type of training he performed in the middle of his off-season. You will notice that he still places emphasis on body control, balance, and mobility during this block of training, but his focus is on exploring his athletic potential.

I needed to master the basics before I earned the right to perform these more complex movements. If you put the time and effort into owning the exercises at the beginning of this book, you will see significantly more progress in the strength and power-focused exercises.

FOCUS ON A DYNAMIC WARM-UP

Once you have progressed through this book and have developed resilience within your body, you can change your preround warm-up to include exercises that will prepare you for not only the upcoming practice or playing session but also future training sessions. If you think about how many preround or preprac- tice warm-ups an avid amateur or professional golfer does, you can appreciate how much of an opportunity the warm-up provides for improving your body over the long term.

In Kevin Chappell's program (table 8.4), we see a section of his pre-golf warm-up. His program normally takes 25 to 30 minutes. One focus of the warm-up is to challenge h is areas of weakness for long-term improvement. The average professional golfer playing 25 to 30 tourna ment weeks will have 125 or more warm-ups per year, and this doesn't include the golf played on off weeks. There is lots of opportunity to improve! The warm-up included in chapter 2 is great for those who are just beginning their journey into fitness, but a more detailed, individualized program involving more complex exercises is appropri- ate as the body improves. In this warm-up , Kevin begins by activating his feet, hips, shoulders, and spine and then moves to full-body exercises that require both rotation and antirotation. He finishes with more dynamic exercises that emphasize speed and use bands to provide progressive resistance. This warm-up provides a nice succession from isolated low-intensity movements to controlled full-body exercises and finally to vigorous high-velocity movements once the body is properly warm and prepared.

The warm-up also gives you a chance to make your deficienciesyour strength. Many of the movements in this warm-up program focus on areas that Kevin wanted to improve in his physical capabilities. If you do the same with your warm-up, you will also notice significant improvements in the way your body is able to move and perform, both on and off the golf course.

Most people who look at my swing think I should make it longer. Luckily,I wasable to find a great coach in Mark Blackbu rn and knowl- edgeable trainers and therapists (the authors of this book) who were able to work with my body to maximize its individual potential. You need to swing the way your body moves most efficiently and not how someone else swings it. It is also important to make sure your body is warmed up for each practice session and round of golf, as a prope r warm-up is more than just a physical activity. Yes, it will help you move more effectively for your round of golf, but it also provides an oppo rtunity to shrug off the variables that are an inescapable aspect of life on the road while creating an incredible opportunity to ensure your body is sufficiently prepa red each and every time you tee it up.

CONCLUSION

We hope you now appreciate what it takes to create a truly effective golf fitness program. Each player's program may differ, even for players at the highest skill levels. Many variables need to be considered when creating an effect ive and efficient fitness program. Golf Anatomy provides a variety of exercises so you can create a fitness program that will better prepare your body for the golf swing. Understanding how the body moves during a proper golf swing allows you to design a fitness program aimed at improving your body's ability to achieve those motions. This is the best way to use fitness to hit the ball farther, more consist- ently, and with more accuracy. We hope Golf Anatomy has given you greater insight into the mechanics of the golf swing and the best way to prepare your body to play better golf.

Made in the USA
Monee, IL
22 May 2022